The Young Riders' Pony Book

Introduced by Debbie Johnsey

The Young Riders' Pony Book

Introduced by
Debbie Johnsey

Edited by Candida Geddes & Dorothy Ward
Ward Lock Ltd. London

Contents

Debbie Johnsey says Hello!

Hello! I'm so glad to be able to talk to you all about my ponies and the fun I've had with them, because I know you must love ponies too, or you wouldn't be reading this book!

I really can't remember a time when I wasn't mad about horses, though I do have a snapshot that shows me looking absolutely terrified of a little Dartmoor pony – I must explain that I was only two at the time! I first started to ride when I was three, on my brother Kevin's pony. Kevin is two years older than I am. After that I just thought about nothing but horses. I sometimes felt school was a dreadful waste of time, but I used to read horsy books and play horsy games and after I left school (because it was getting so difficult to fit all my riding in and go to school as well) I had a tutor for a while. I always liked English, mathematics and French and in fact I am going on teaching myself French now, because I should like to be really fluent in it.

When I was beginning to ride, we lived on the outskirts of a town and we didn't have anywhere near the house where we could keep horses. My father rented a field about two miles away and I used to walk there or take my saddle on my bike. My first pony was a Welsh Mountain called Silver; we still have Silver now and we have had 5 foals out of her. Then my father bought me a little hunting pony that had jumped a bit. His name was Stephen, and with him I started to get really interested in jumping. I used to put up jumps for myself, using broomsticks balanced on buckets. My next two ponies were Nosey Parker and Tango, both 12.2s. Tango was the first pony that I really schooled for myself. I was eight at that time. I started him in the winter and by the middle of the next summer we won the Martini junior jumping championship of Wales. But he wasn't always so obliging; he once threw me three times at the first fence!

When I was nearly ten I had my first 14.2, Spider, who was a real rogue. He would jump beautifully one day and refuse everything the next. He loved to rear up on his back legs! He won a couple of classes, but we only kept him about a year. My next 14.2,

Lady Ennis, was a Grade JA Irish, and we won a few local shows, but I had a fairly serious accident when she fell on me and my lung was punctured. I had to go into hospital for a week and have a sort of tube inside me, but I managed to get back to jumping after about three weeks, so I was lucky.

Then I saw a 14.2 novice pony called Champ and I liked the look of him so much that I was overjoyed when my mother bought him for me. We sold the others and within two weeks of jumping him, Champ, who was every bit as good as I had hoped, was JA'd. After that he won most of his classes. He had an annoying taste for stopping in doubles, but he did not take long to get over that. Then we sold Nosey Parker and kept Tango, so I had him for 12.2s and Champ for 14.2s. Champ is really a super pony. I have a beautiful portrait of him, that hangs over the mantlepiece at home.

One day I was at Wembley – only watching, because I had *just* missed qualifying – when we saw a lovely pony called Mystery. He was doing quite well, but my father and I thought we could improve him and we were able to buy him. He did have some problems, as he had at some time been frightened and was apt to bolt, but I started schooling him and it only took from Easter to July, and then he was able to take a first at Hickstead.

When I was eleven, Champ and I were picked for the Junior European International Championships. We couldn't ride in them – but that's another story you can read later on in this book!

By the time I was fourteen my father thought I had done well enough to change from ponies to horses. This is a difficult change, partly because ponies are so much brighter than horses – they think for themselves and often help their riders out of difficulties. With a horse you have to do all the thinking! So we turned Champ out for a year, after which Clair, my sister, took him over.

Speculator and Red Paul were two horses we bought. Red Paul went well but I found I had some trouble with Speculator. However, my father bought Kingfisher and riding him helped me with Speculator, who started going really well. We came second in the National Adults and second in the Leading Show Jumper, which Ann Moore won. So we sold Red Paul and kept Speculator and Kingfisher. Of course it was on Speculator that I won the European Junior Championship, and the Leading Young Rider of Great Britain and the Young Rider's Championship of Great Britain, the Leading Lady Rider at St. Gallen in Switzerland and the Babycham Gold Cup at the Bath and West.

Now I have two super American horses, Assam

and Croupier. Assam's grandfather was Mahmoud, who made the fastest time ever in the Derby. He is a really well bred thoroughbred on the lines of Mill Reef. His sire is Jaipur, who is by Nasrullah whose sire was Nearco. He's a dark chestnut. Although he's a novice, he's not a complete beginner, because he has done hunting classes in the United States. I think both he and Croupier have got a great future and I hope we shall have lots of successes together. Last year I had to rest Speculator because he had injured his back, but Assam and I won the Wills Embassy Stakes at Hickstead with Frederick Broome, David's young brother, coming second.

So now you know about my horses; later on in the book you can read more about me and my friends.

Eventing

Many people think that eventing is the most testing competition of all for both horses and riders. To succeed in completing the three days of a big three-day event, you need a high-quality horse, trained with knowledge and skill to the peak of fitness. The horse must be calm and obedient enough to perform a dressage test smoothly and accurately, have the stamina, speed and jumping ability to cope with the speed and endurance phase on the second day, and be fit and sound enough to pass the veterinary examination on the third day and go on to complete a show-jumping course.

It is the second day of three-day events that provides the most interesting horsemanship to watch, and which is the greatest test of horse and rider. There are several different phases in this part of the competition, starting with about four miles over roads and tracks at a walk and trot or gentle canter, followed by a steeplechase course, more roads and tracks and then, after only a moment's pause, straight into the cross-country course–up to five miles long and with between thirty and forty big, solid fences to be jumped. In all, horse and rider will have travelled up to twenty-five miles, within a time limit.

When you watch the best international riders competing in a three-day event, they sometimes make it look so easy that you forget the months of training and preparation that have gone into getting the horse ready for the competition. And sometimes, of course, not even the experts succeed. All major competitions are stiff enough for only the best horses and most skilled riders to get through without being penalised.

Since the second world war, when three-day events have become so popular, one-day events and competitions at Pony Club level are also held. For anybody with a good, all-round pony and a certain amount of experience, one-day events can be very rewarding competitions to go in for. They can be great fun to ride in, and they show how good your all-rounder really is. There are lots of young riders whose ponies happily compete in hunter trials and show jumping competitions, and the dressage test at this level is quite easy if your pony is properly schooled. A Pony Club event may be some way from the big three-day events, but the essentials are all there, it's very good experience–and where many of today's top competitors began!

Skookum

a story by Carol Vaughan

I chose this story and the one on page 64 because
I love Westerns, and I am sure you do, too

"Bob's roping a horse for you in the corral," Kay called to her twelve year old sister.

It was Jill's first visit to her brother-in-law's cattle ranch and it was very different from England. Climbing to the top bar of the corral she saw Bob standing inside with the herd of saddle-horses milling round him, a lariat in his hand.

"Hi," he shouted. "I'm just getting a pony out for you." He swung the rope into a whirling loop and it snaked out, falling cleanly round the neck of a big, brown pony.

Bob coiled up the slack and led him over. The pony had bright eyes, a shock of tangled mane and a long, thick tail. "This is a good one," Bob said. "He's an Indian mustang, raised on the Reservation. My young brother, Jeff, did the tribe a good turn and the Chief sent Skookum as a present. 'Skookum' is Indian for 'plenty good' and this pony is as cute as they come. Jeff taught him to bow and lie down like a circus pony, and he can work cattle, too. I guess you'll like him."

As he spoke he bridled the pony and cinched on a heavy western stock saddle, complete with its coiled lariat. Jill mounted and rode Skookum round while Bob quickly roped and saddled a big sorrel for himself.

"We are going to ride over to the main herd," said Bob; "I am going on to Ropside Range to look at some stock but that is too far for your first day, so we will take Flint and he will guide you home again." He whistled and the big Alsatian, who was sitting in the kitchen doorway watching Kay make a meat pie for supper, tore himself reluctantly away.

Bob held the sorrel to a jog trot, sitting easily in the saddle and Jill, watching him, remembered not to 'rise' and soon found the easy rhythm of Skookum's gait less tiring than a trot. They forded the river which ran through a wooded valley and reached the low grass hills of the range. Bob reined in on a ridge overlooking a big, shallow valley where hundreds of white-faced cattle grazed on the rich, green grass, watched by a lone cowboy.

"Hi...aa!" yelled Bob. Some of the steers raised their heads

briefly and returned to the more important business of eating, but the cowboy came at a gallop. "Hi, Jake," said Bob. "Rode out to look over things. This is Kay's sister, Jill, out from England. We're making a cowgirl of her. Jill, this is Jake Walk-in-the-Door."

The dark Indian boy smiled and said, "Howdy, Jill."

"Anything been happening?" asked Bob.

"Yeah," drawled Jake. "Lorst a cow and a calf. Cow musta strayed from the herd. Came bustin' out of the brush, lickety split and broke a laig. Tried to backtrack her, but lorst the trail down by the river. Cain't figger what scared her into leavin' the calf, lessen it was already daid. Will be now, anyways. Heard cougar, the other night."

Bob shrugged his shoulders. "Guess we'll have to cross them off the tally," he said. "Look, I want you to ride up to Topside with me this morning. Jill will ride home with Flint for company. Guess she'll be safe enough."

"Skookum take her home," grinned Jake. "Good pony, plenty savvy."

Flint bounded after Jill when she rode off homewards and then stopped, looking doubtfully back at his master. "Good dog, go with Jill," encouraged Bob, and the dog soon settled down to escort her home, running in wide circles round the brown pony, casting for exciting scents to investigate.

They had reached the ford when Jill heard the dog barking upstream. Skookum pricked his ears and turned to stare. Flint appeared between the trees, barked and ran back again. Jill turned her pony and rode up the narrow, riverside track. Above the ford the river was less wide but much faster, bubbling and churning on its stony bed. Flint was quivering with excitement on the river bank and barking at a tiny island in mid-stream, which was apparently deserted; except for three small trees, a tiny patch of close-cropped grass and a tangle of bushes.

"There's nothing there," said Jill. "What are you making all this fuss about?"

"Woof," insisted Flint, jumping up and down with impatience and pawing at the water. Suddenly he ran upstream and, after a moment's hesitation, launched himself into the swiftly running current. Swimming strongly, he made enough headway for the river to sweep him up onto the island. Running to the tangle of bushes, he prodded something Jill could not see, with his nose, and then to bark again, insistently.

Jill, her curiosity really aroused, copied Flint's tactics, by riding upstream and forcing the reluctant pony into the river. Sliding out of the saddle, clinging to the horn, she pulled Skookum's rein, pushing his head out into mid-stream, and managed to reach the island.

Wagging his tail, Flint leaped towards them and then ran back to his find. It was the missing calf, very tiny and very cold, but still breathing. The calf needed warmth and food without delay and Jill wondered how she could possibly take it back. If she tied the dead weight of the calf to the saddle, the pony might sink in the fast current. Slowly she thought out a plan. Fetching the lariat from her saddle, she made the calf a dog's harness, with the 'lead' fastened on front of his chest. Then she half dragged, half carried him to the edge of the island and, coiling the remaining part of the lariat, she tried to throw it to the river bank. Twice it tangled itself up and fell in the water, but the third time the end caught in a projecting tree root and held firm. Launching Skookum from the downstream end of the island, they struggled back to the shore, landing far down, very wet and blown.

Leading the pony back along the bank, Jill rescued the lariat, hitched the end to the saddlehorn and said, "Now, Skookum, back. Back, boy." Holding his bridle, she made him take the strain and pull on the rope. With a splash the calf slid off the island, followed by the excited Flint. Jill kept backing the pony and, with the current helping, the calf came ashore with a jerk. Leaving Skookum holding the rope taut, she ran to the bank and hauled the calf onto dry land. Skookum, a trained cowpony, backed again as soon as he felt the rope slacken and the calf came up with a rush, knocking Jill over and landing on her lap. "Whoa, Skoojum! Whoa!" shouted Jill, when she had recovered her breath, trying to crawl free of the calf.

Jill wondered if Skookum had forgotten his circus tricks as she led him close to the limp calf. Remembering circus acts she had seen, Jill broke a long, thin switch from a tree. Holding the pony's rein, she tapped him behind his knee. "Down, Skookum! Bow!" she ordered. Jill had to repeat the order several times, tapping him behind his knee, before Skookum hesitantly dropped to his knees. Jill patted him in delight and kept reassuring him with her voice, while she picked the calf up by his harness and lifted him across the saddle.

Working fast, she tied the calf's legs to the broad stirrup leathers and held on firmly as she said, "Up, Skookum." The pony scrambled to his feet, snorting with surprise at his strange burden and Jill used the last length of the lariat to tie the calf to the saddle. There was not much room for her in the saddle, but she managed to squeeze on behind the calf, standing in her stirrups and leaning backwards. She rode home at a cautious amble, afraid that the calf might slip, but all her makeshift knots held. As the movement warmed his body the calf bawled a weak but decided protest against horse-riding. Jill patted his nose.

"You'll soon be home now," she told him. "We'll find you some nice warm milk and then you'll feel fine."

Kay heard Flint barking madly and when she saw the strange cavalcade through the window she came rushing out, calling to one of the cowbows to come and help. Jill explained what had happened while they untied the calf.

"You mean you swam out to the island and toted it all the way home by yourself?" said the cowboy incredulously.

"I didn't think there was time to fetch help. He was so cold and he looked so sick," explained Jill.

The cowboy grinned. "Nothing wrong with the little fella that some grub won't cure," he drawled and lifting the calf clear of the saddle he carried him away.

Jill leaned wearily against her tired pony, feeling as limp as the calf now that the excitement was over.

"What an exciting morning you have had," said Kay. "What do you think of ranch life now?"

"Plenty good," replied Jill laughing. "Skookum!"

Buying a Pony

by Candida Geddes

There are some points that **are** worth remembering whether the pony you are thinking of buying is your first or just one in a long list of them. Obviously, if you have bought a pony before you will know some of the ways of going about it, even if you did not have to learn the hard way by discovering that you had made a mistake.

The first thing to ask yourself is whether you—or your parents—can afford to keep a pony at all. Owning a pony can be very expensive, and always costs much more than you think. It is no good hoping that if you keep your pony in a field he will just look after himself all the year round. He will need some sort of shelter, and a constant supply of water. These will have to be provided by you if they are not there already. You will also need to buy grooming things, and tack for the pony and equipment for yourself. All you need yourself is the right sort of footwear and a hard hat, but if you want to join the Pony Club, go in for gymkhanas, competitions and so on, you will need proper riding clothes which, even if you buy them second hand, still cost quite a lot. During the winter your pony will need extra feeding, and if you are going to work him at all hard, this will apply all the year round. And what about vet's bills, blacksmith's bills, and all the other extras?

Once you have taken all these financial horrors into your thoughts and have still remained determined to have a pony, you need to think about two more things before going out in search of the right one. Where are you going to keep your pony? This is important. If you live in the country, you should be able to find a farmer who will let you pay to keep your pony in one of his fields. If you live in a village or a small town this is also most likely to be the best solution. If you live in a big town you may have to be prepared to travel quite a long way to see your pony. What you must not do is think that a pony can live happily in a back garden or a tiny orchard. Even if the pony himself is not actually very big he needs quite a lot of space, and it really is cruel not to allow a big enough area for the pony to move around in freely. Needless to say, keeping your pony in the garden shed is no good, either. Horses kept in stables are rather different, because they have intensive schooling and exercise every day and get a good deal more attention than you are likely to be able to devote to your pony.

This leads on to that second important thought. How much time can you, or will you, spend with your pony? Will you go and see him every day? Will you ride him regularly—not just occasionally when it's a sunny day and you feel like exploring, but when it is wet and cold and what you really would like to do is to curl up by the fire with a book, or watch television? Make sure you are going to enjoy your pony in spite of the drawbacks before you decide to spend any of that money we have talked about.

Enough about the possible snags and problems. The last thing we want to do is put you off, but for the pony's sake as well as your own it is important you know what you are letting yourself in for by buying your first pony.

When you start to look for a pony to buy there are several things to remember. First of all, make sure that somebody who really knows a lot about horses will help you to choose yours. Choosing a pony that is good and is right for you—which is not necessarily the same thing—is not always easy. So don't be too shy to ask for advice, which a riding school instructor, Pony Club official or other expert will always be glad to provide for you. Try to find a pony that you already know: perhaps one that a friend has grown out of. Do, though, make sure that you and the friend are at about the same riding standard. If you are quite a novice, a spirited pony that goes beautifully for your friend might just become difficult to control with a less experienced rider on its back. Alternatively, if you have ridden a lot you will not find it exciting and challenging enough to ride a pony that is half asleep all the time. This applies, of course, to any pony you are thinking of buying, not just one belonging to a friend!

When you go to try a pony, get somebody else to ride it before you do. Does the pony look friendly when it is approached, or does it put back its ears and roll its eyes? Is it obedient? Does it move away from 'home' as readily as it does when turned towards the stables? Does it respond to the aids promptly, without having to be yanked in the mouth and dug in the ribs? Will it jump? If you want to jump but are not experienced enough to cope with a pony that has never seen a pole in its path before, you need to ask the question now.

Now it is your turn. Approach the pony and talk to it, begin to make friends with it. When you mount does it stand still, or does it either trot off with you clutching on, or turn round and try to nip you? We seem to be painting a potentially very black picture. Of course it doesn't matter if a pony has some bad habits, but if it has been thoroughly spoilt it will be very difficult to break the habits, and bad habits can turn into real vices, so just be careful.

How does the pony feel when you are riding it? Is it comfortable or jerky, does it go well for you, or did it behave well with its owner on top but misbehave abominably with you? Ride the pony long enough to begin to get the feel of it walking, trotting and cantering. The most important question of all is DO YOU LIKE THE PONY? No matter how suitable a pony appears to be, it will be no good buying it if you don't think you will become friends.

As well as being an important clue to the pony's ability to move and jump well, its conformation – the right way to describe how a pony is constructed – will affect its health and strength. Horses with bad conformation are more likely to suffer from strains, jolts, all sorts of minor ailments. And a pony with good conformation will look much nicer, too. Does he stand foursquare, your possible pony? Is his chest broad enough and his girth deep enough for there to be plenty of room for his lungs and heart to expand, or, if you stand in front of him, does he look as though his front legs come out of one hole? Is his expression alert, are his eyes kind and shining (the first will tell you about his temperament; the second about his state of health). Are his legs strong and straight, does his shoulder slope, are his quarters nicely rounded or do they fall away to nothing? How about his feet? Feet are terribly important. The best way to learn about conformation at first hand is to watch. Go to a show and study the judging of show pony classes, especially the novice classes. At the big shows, the ponies may all be of such high quality that it is difficult to see any very big difference between them, but the novice classes will show you what the judges think important about a pony before it has been so fully schooled that some of its defects – and no pony is perfect – are hardly noticeable. The judge won't be looking only for the best conformation (as you will find out if you turn to page 73) but it is an important part of judging. The day you yourself pick the winner, and are fairly sure you know why it was chosen, you can go out and look for your pony by yourself.

When you find the pony you want get the vet to look at it. Vets do not give certificates of soundness any more, as they used to be unfairly blamed when a certified horse later went lame, but a good vet will give the pony a thorough inspection and tell you if anything seems to be wrong. Lastly, ask to have the pony on trial for a week or so. It is a perfectly reasonable request, and if the answer is not a cheerful 'Yes', you might be wise to have second thoughts about buying it!

Different Ponies and Different Jumps

Here's a mixture of jumps and ponies. Starting from the left there's Tango at Ebbw Vale when I was 8 or 9; then Tango in his first proper jumping class. Next comes Mystery on one of the first times I rode him, at Hickstead. Underneath is Sea Gem in his first class as a complete novice; and Champ at Windsor. The bottom row has Champ again, winning the North of England Championship; with Silver King as a novice at Barry Show and Nosey Parker winning at Chepstow when I was ten

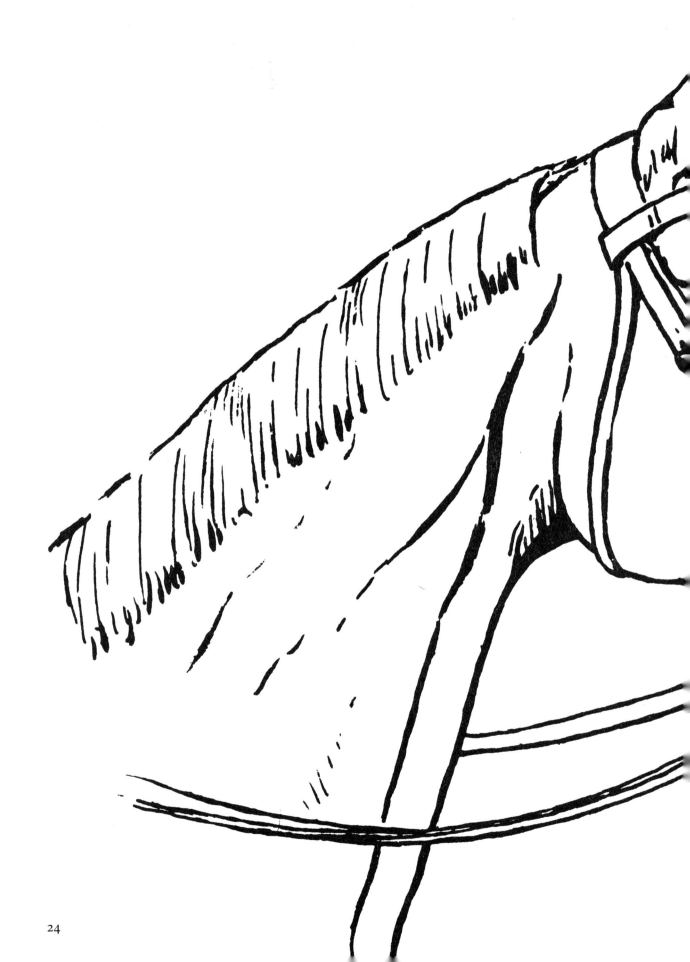

Saddlery

by Candida Geddes

If you go into a saddler's shop you will find a bewildering variety of equipment, from rugs to martingales, brushing boots to blinkers. For the ordinary pony, most of these things won't be necessary, but it's probably a good thing if you know about most of them.

What you will need for your pony is a bridle that fits, with a bit of the right size and right sort; a saddle which is comfortable for the pony and for you; a headcollar and rope. Of course, you will need grooming kit, buckets and so on, but let's just concentrate on tack for the moment. If you are buying a pony for the first time, it is as well to ask whether the pony's tack is for sale too. Make sure that it is in good condition, and not worn or cracked. Pay particular attention to stitching, and to the stuffing of the saddle (you can have it restuffed if necessary). If you are thinking of buying tack, try to get good second-hand equipment. Most saddlers sell second-hand things, and apart from saving some money you will—if it has been properly looked after—have tack that is supple and a nice dark colour. New tack needs a good deal of attention, as the leather is usually stiff and uncomfortable to wear at first.

The fit of your saddle and bridle is extremely important. Think how you feel in a pair of shoes that are too tight—the pony will feel the same if his tack does not fit. The bridle should fit snugly, the bit lying comfortable in the mouth, just wrinkling the corners of his lips. The noseband should be roomy, the throatlatch loose enough to allow the breadth of four fingers between it and the pony's jaw, the browband and headpiece so positioned that the pony's ears are not constricted. The saddle should fit neatly in the dip of the pony's back, the pommel *well clear* of the withers even when the weight of the rider is added on top, and not so narrow as to pinch the sides of the withers. The saddle must rest clear of the spine along all its length, and not be so long that it sits on the pony's loins. If you are in any doubt about the way your tack fits, do ask an expert rather than risk riding your pony in discomfort. He is likely to become unco-operative and bad-tempered—and can you blame him!

What bit is best for your pony? Unless he immediately becomes uncontrollable and carts you off into the far distance whenever he can, keep to the rule of: the simpler the better. If your pony goes well in a simple snaffle, don't put him into a Pelham just because you think it looks smarter. There was a time when a good deal of nonsense was talked about finding the 'key' to a horse's mouth. Some difficult horses do need to be ridden in complex headgear, but on the whole the more complicated the bit, the less desirable the horse. A horse that goes well, calmly and happily in a snaffle with no adornments is either sleepy, or well trained, obedient and altogether to be admired.

Stirrup irons: the standard type (left) and the safety iron.

Some ponies are decidedly headstrong, and do need a bit that is slightly stronger than a plain snaffle. The addition of a drop noseband can often do the trick, though this needs very special care when it is being fitted, or it can do a good deal of harm. A lot of ponies go extremely well in a Pelham, though nobody quite knows why as it breaks all the rules of the theory of bitting! Only use a double bridle if your pony already goes well and kindly in a snaffle, if you have had quite a lot of experience and if you really understand what the effect of the double is and how to use it. It is a great mistake to think that your pony's head carriage and behaviour will miraculously be transformed if you put two bits in his mouth instead of one.

If your pony constantly carries his head up so high that you bang your nose, and no amount of schooling makes any difference – and with excitable ponies a lot of skill is needed to break them of the habit – you may need a martingale. There are two principal kinds: the 'standing' martingale, which attaches to the girth at one end, passes through the neckstrap and fixes on to the noseband (*not* a drop noseband) at the other end; and the 'running' martingale,

which divides after it has passed through the neckstrap so the reins can pass through a ring on each end. If you are using a running martingale, make sure that you have leather or rubber stops fixed on to the reins between the bit and the martingale rings. If the rings ever catch on the bit – and they can do so, without the stops – you will find yourself in a very nasty mess. A martingale must be fitted so that it in no way restricts the pony's head movement until it gets up really high, but it must not be so loose that the pony can catch his feet in it.

There seem to be a lot of do's and don'ts in this piece. It is not really as difficult as it may sound, but for the pony's comfort and your safety it really is very important that everything is made to fit properly, and that you understand why you use a particular kind of equipment. And once you have got it, make sure you look after it carefully. Saddlery should be kept clean and have saddle soap rubbed well in to the leather to keep it supple; serge or linen panels must be regularly brushed; and so on. If you care for your tack, it will last until long after you have outgrown both it and your pony.

My mother used to sing this song to me when I was little. I always loved it, but it made me cry.

A Bridle Hanging on the Wall

There's a bridle hanging on the wall,
It's the one that my old pony wore.
No more he answers to my call
For that bridle hanging on the wall.

There's a horseshoe nailed upon the door,
It's the one that my old pony wore.
No more he answers to my call
For that horseshoe nailed upon the wall.

There's a blanket laid out on the stall,
It's the one that my old pony wore
No more he answers to my call
For that blanket laid out on the stall.

From my pony to my guide
I used to ride along the trail
Watching the sun setting.
But now my good old pony's gone
To where the good old ponies go,
That's the land so far, so far away.

Saddlery Quiz

How many saddles and bridles do you recognise? Find the answers on page 77

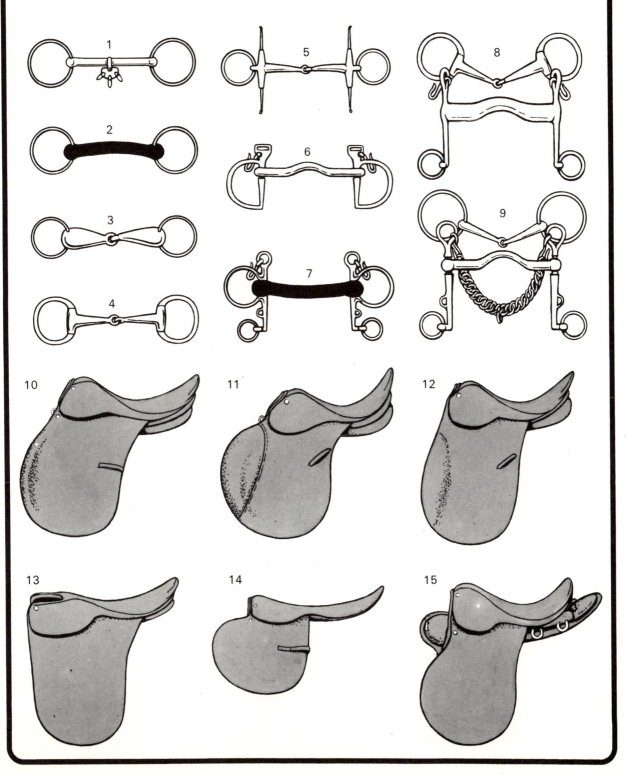

Me and My Family

by Debbie Johnsey

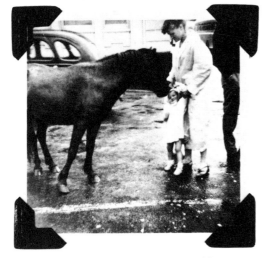

The first time I met a pony I was scared!

Jumping off with two ponies we only had one set of studs, my father helped me to change them.

I live with my family in a house right in the middle of the country, with a super view of the Severn in the distance. The house used to be a cottage, but we had it enlarged–there are six of us and we take up quite a lot of room!–and of course my father has built stables for the horses, including the racehorses and the ponies. Quite often during the season I go with my father to the races to watch our horses run, and I always enjoy that.

I really don't read anything much except books about horses, and I can't get hold of enough of those. I like stories about racing and show jumping, of course, and biographies and autobiographies of show-jumping people like Pat Smythe. I loved Black Beauty, in spite of it making me cry, and I used to read all the children's books I could lay my hands on about ponies and gymkhanas.

I generally go to the cinema about once a week when I'm at home–that is provided there's a good film on. I need hardly tell you that my favourite films at the cinema or on TV are Westerns, with lots of horses and ponies galloping through deserts and mountains. Keeping fit is one of my obsessions, too. I play squash and I love athletics and running. I don't do any formal training, but I run everywhere! I do press-ups to keep me in shape and I love swimming, too, but unfortunately I don't get as much as I should like, because I am busy non-stop all through the summer. Once I was lucky because my parents, who were going to Jamaica, decided to take me and a friend of mine

and not only was I able to swim in the gorgeous warm sea, I also had the luck to meet Donovan, who was staying with his wife and little boy in the same place. Donovan is one of my favourite pop stars, and I like John Denver, David Cassidy, the Osmonds and Elton John. I've been listening to Leo Sayer and David Essex, too, and I think they're both fabulous.

I often think how lucky I am to have the opportunity to ride as much as I want to, and to belong to a family who are all mad about horses– even my mother loves them although she doesn't ride herself. My father was a National Hunt jockey, so he helps me and advises me all the time; and now

My first Championship on Mystery

that he is breeding racehorses I am allowed to help to train them and gallop them.

I mentioned before, how I was chosen for the Junior European Team the first time. There were about 18 competitors and we had to assemble at Hickstead at ten-o'-clock. Douglas Bunn, who owns Hickstead, rang a big bell and asked all the children

That's me on Nosey Parker in the top picture, and underneath it you can see Clair on Champ.

and their parents to gather round and listen to him. He told us that it was a big course – bigger than the championship course – and he just wanted us to go in and jump as well as we could, but anybody who wanted to could back out. (My mother says that at this point she felt like taking me home again, because it all sounded so formidable!) Anybody who came near to jumping the course would be asked to jump again.

I had to go in about 7th, on Champ. Two of my friends had already had bad rounds, but my father

would never let me watch other people – if you see your friends in trouble it's worrying and depressing and makes you feel sort of hopeless before you start. Our friend Ted Edgar came up just as I was going in and put his arm round me and said, 'Just keep riding. That pony can do it.' He was right – Champ was the only one to jump a clear round.

Clair, Lee, and me with Kingfisher.

Afterwards we all went to the Clubhouse and the team was announced. Douglas Bunn said that Champ was definitely first choice 'on his brilliant performance today.' You can guess how proud I felt. I knew he was good, but I hadn't realised quite *how* good! That made me the youngest person in any sport to be picked to represent Great Britain.

During the next three weeks we were busy getting passports and so on, but then they found some old rule that said members of the team must be at least 14 – and I was 11! I remember my father said 'Come in here a minute, I've something to tell you. Don't be too upset.' I was really worried because I thought it might be something wrong with one of the ponies! I was disappointed, of course, who wouldn't be? but one of my first thoughts was: 'Well at any rate now I shall be able to go to Blackpool for the National Championship.' I managed to win that on Mystery, and next year on Champ and the year after on Mystery again. Mystery won it again a couple of years later with his new owner, so I was pleased to think that my ponies had won it four years out of five.

Horses in Australia

In Australia you can find large numbers of horses that have been imported from other parts of the world, and also some uniquely Australian breeds. The equestrian sports in Australia also include events not found in other parts of the world as well as the ones that are popular in other places.

The most important and popular of the Australian breeds is the Waler. His origins are obscure, though it is known that he is descended from various sources, most importantly the Cape Horses of South Africa with a dash of English Thoroughbred. The Waler was recently given the official name of the Australian Stockhorse, a job which the breed is very well equipped to do. The Waler is a smallish horse, about 15 to 15.2 hands, with a close-coupled body, specially strong legs and feet, a long-ranging, free stride, and enough stamina to keep him going all day in the outback. The Waler is the most popular breed in Australia for endurance rides, and he makes an ideal mount for this competition.

The Waler has been popular for cattle work for many years, but the Quarter Horse, imported from the United States, is also proving himself, as this breed, too, has agility and stamina and the intelligence so necessary if a horse is really going to help with the cattle.

Racing is a passion of the Australians, so it is hardly surprising that more Thoroughbreds are being imported, and being bred in Australia itself as well. Some people feel that the climate of New

Zealand and its green pastures can offer a better environment for Thoroughbreds than can Australia. The Arabian horse, another popular breed, should, however, find itself at home in the harsher conditions of Australia.

Appaloosas can be found in Australia, as can the high-stepping American Saddlebred, which is mainly used for breeding purposes. You can see hackney horses and ponies from Britain, and other harness horses which have been imported for the driving classes at shows. The heavy breeds can also be found in the show ring, but they are not much in demand for work.

All sorts of activities for children and ponies are available in Australia, and while the Australian ponies are attractive and handy animals, some of the British pony breeds are also much in demand, particularly the Welsh ponies and the Shetland.

Apart from endurance riding and racing, there are many other sporting events in Australia. Rodeos are held, quite rightly in a country where the cattleman and his horse play an important part; polo is played, and an Australian variation of it called polocrosse, which provides all the fun and excitement but is a much less expensive game, as each player needs only one horse. There are one- and three-day events, too; Australian three-day event teams have done extremely well in international competitions (the Gold Medal at the 1960 Olympic Games was won by Lawrence Morgan on Salad Days). There are trotting and pacing races, 'picnic' as well as the more formal race meetings, high-jumping in the show ring, and a host of other events at shows, ranging from in-hand showing classes to colourful costume classes and gymkhana events.

Gymkhana Events

Games on horseback have been played for thousands of years all over the world. Originally they were part of the training needed as a preparation for war; now, gymkhana events are still good training, even if the aim is less serious.

All sorts of different ponies are good at gymkhana events. It is not necessary to have a well-bred show pony in order to have fun–and even to win. What is more important is enough practice at home before you get to a gymkhana, and a pony which knows what he is meant to be doing. Gymkhana events are really a matter of timing. If your pony can stop dead, move off at a canter from a halt, turn on a tight circle and so on, you are half way there. So put up a row of bending poles at home, and practise riding through them, weaving from side to side in order to go round the poles, but trying to go in as straight a line as possible. Teach your pony to make a fast start by practising going from a walk to a canter without trotting in between–and this does *not* mean just giving your pony a great kick and a shout and hoping for the best. Make sure he is concentrating, get him to move forward in an energetic walk and then ask him to canter. Once he has got the idea, it should not be too difficult to teach him to move off quickly from a halt.

Some gymkhana events involve flags, balloons and other unfamiliar things. Before you enter a gymkhana, make sure that your pony does not mind them, nor noises like the rattle a potato makes when you drop it in a bucket. And will your pony lead properly? There is nothing more annoying than teaching yourself to run fast inside a sack, and then to find that your pony is so horrified by what you are doing that he refuses to come with you!

A quick, nimble and obedient pony and lots of practice by yourself and with friends, and you should do well. Remember, though, that enjoying yourself is more important than winning, and make sure that your pony is enjoying himself too.

I went in for several gymkhanas when I was 7 or 8 — and they were great fun. The first thing I ever won was the musical sack race.

What your Pony Thinks

by Candida Geddes

If you and your pony are to be friends, it is important for you to understand some of the things that make him behave in the way he does. A pony that is frightened will probably be difficult to relax with; one that has been allowed its own way all the time won't be any fun at all.

It is quite likely that all the ponies you know have been brought up surrounded by people, safe and snug in fields or stables, with enough food and drink always there, and nothing at all to worry about. But it has not always been like this. For thousands of years ponies lived in a very different way, in wild herds. The herd would have to look after itself—nobody appeared with buckets of oats for *them*!—which meant finding enough food, and protecting themselves from enemies in the form of other wild animals. Ponies now have not forgotten their tougher days, and the herd instinct is still one of the strongest instincts in ponies and in horses. Ponies always prefer being in groups, and are often nervous and lonely by themselves. This is because in their wild state they had to keep together for protection, and it is a lesson they have never forgotten.

Being somewhere that they know is also important for horses and ponies. If you buy a new pony it will probably be restless for a few days after it first comes to live with you, even if there are other ponies in the field with it. This is because anywhere strange might, the pony thinks, be frightening. Ponies like to have a home. Part of feeling comfortable is having enough to eat. If you do have a new pony, or if you take your pony somewhere strange, soothe him by feeding him yourself, even if you only pluck grass and give it to him. It all helps him to relax.

Ponies that live in—in other words ones that are usually stabled—will want to return to their stables when they are away from them. Have you ever noticed ponies leaving their own stable very lazily and, when they start on the journey home, becoming much more keen? This is part of needing security, and partly, too, the fact that getting home again probably means it is time for a meal—so greed comes into it, too.

If you want your pony to concentrate, which you will if you are schooling him or teaching him to jump, for example, it is a good idea to find somewhere for this which is not *too* close to home. It is not always possible, but if you have a choice, don't school your pony in the field he lives in, or in the field next to his stable. There are few things more annoying than a pony which will not concentrate because he is longing to get back to his stable. On the other hand, and particularly if you are helping to school a young pony, it is a good idea to let him get used to the field where you are going to do the schooling. If the field is quite strange to him, he will probably snort his way past the hedge and find it difficult to concentrate again–this time because he is on the lookout for danger of some sort.

A word of warning, though. It is usually quite easy to tell whether a pony is frightened or is being obstinate. *Never* get cross with a pony who is being disobedient through fear, you will only make him more nervous in the future. On the other hand, ponies can be stubborn and self-willed, so it is a mistake *always* to give in to them. Discipline is important for a pony, and he must respect you. In fact it's almost true to say that it is a mistake ever to give in to your pony–but don't get cross with him. Be firm, but be reasonable, and only growl at him if he is being disobedient out of obstinacy,

rather than because he is frightened or doesn't understand what you want him to do.

This leads us on to another thing–if you are asking your pony to do anything, and specially if it is something new, make quite sure he understands what you are getting at. It is all too easy to give muddled instructions and then get cross because the pony isn't doing what you ask. Before you blame him, stop and think whether you really made yourself clear enough for him to understand.

Most ponies want to be helpful and to please. They are usually very friendly and co-operative. Get to know your pony before asking him to do anything–make friends, in other words. Talk to your pony, because talking will give him confidence. Find out what his odd characteristics are. Some ponies are terrified of donkeys; others love them. Some get frightened over pieces of paper blowing around, or puddles of water, or all sorts of harmless things. Some ponies are ticklish, and enjoy being tickled; others are ticklish and hate being tickled!

Really the important thing to remember is that your pony is in some ways like a person. No two people are exactly the same, and ponies, too, are all different.

POINTS OF THE HORSE

How many points of the horse do you know?
Add as many labels as you can to the picture
shown here. To find out any that you do not
know, look on page 77.

My Friends and Rivals

These are my main rivals in the Junior Jumping world, but they are my friends, too, and as you can see, we jump together as a team. I have known all of them for at least six years and I know from experience that if I go in first in a jump-off and have any one of these behind me, I have to be really fast and clear

top   *Lindsay Vaughan on that very good, genuine pony Nutcracker. That's one pony I have always thought a lot of; and one that is always in the line-up*

left   *Amanda Bakewell on Star Flight*
When Amanda makes a clear round it is always a fast one. Mandy and Star Flight are always there for the really big courses

left   *Lynne Chapman on Dunardee*
I have met Lynne in 12.2's as well as 14.2's and she always provides strong opposition for me. Now my little sister, Clair, competes against her little sister, Julie

bottom   *Pat Kaye on Pierrot*
Pat comes from the North and is probably one of the strongest opposition ever in Junior Jumping. When there was a five days' jumping she would win one day and I would win the next

top right   *The Junior European Championship team in Belgium in 1973*
Janet Randall on Xanthos; Lindsay Vaughan on Fanny Hill; Penny Wilson on Kartoffel; Victoria Turner on Damask and me on Speculator

bottom right   *The Junior European Championship team at Hickstead in 1971*
Nicky Paine on Merry Widow; Rebecca Richardson on Relincho; Ann Colman on Havana Royal and me on Champ. Mr Gerald Barnes is the Chef d'Equipe

Carts, Coaches and Carriages

Man learned a very long time ago that a horse or pony could pull a bigger load behind it than it could carry on its back. Once the wheel was invented it can't have been a big step to discover that humans might travel in the cart. Chariots pulled by horses were used in war and for races by ancient peoples.

Between these early days and the eighteenth century various horse-drawn vehicles for carrying about both goods and people were used. Then, in the eighteenth century, driving began to gain popularity as a sport, and more attention was paid to the appearance of the vehicle itself. As these became lighter and less cumbersome, so the horses could be selected for their appearance – it became very important to have a smart turnout – and even their speed, rather than needing to rely just on strength. The roads which, since the days of the Romans, had been neglected until they became rivers of mud in winter and rutted tracks in summer, were being improved at last.

The very first mail coach ran from Bath to London in 1784, and made such an impression that mail coaches soon became a way of life. The horses were changed every ten miles or so along the way, so the mails could reach their destination with all possible speed. Soon after the mail coaches became established, stage coaches also made their mark. The mail coach could carry four passengers, and the advantages of making money by transporting travellers were quickly realised. The road coaches, as stage coaches were sometimes called, carried twelve passengers for a slightly lower fare. The days of 'public transport' in England had begun.

Once driving had become a sport as well as a necessity, people began to pay more attention to the vehicle itself. During the nineteenth century many different types of carriage were introduced, and although driving declined when the railways were introduced, the sport has now revived and become so popular in the last few years that you can now see many of the old vehicles again – dog-carts, landaus, gigs, curricles, phaetons, governess carts and many more. And not only if you live in England, either, for both horses, harness and various types of carriages, beautifully restored, are exported from Britain to other parts of the world where driving is also a popular sport.

It's a Wild West World

Westerns are definitely my favourite kind of film and I never miss one if I can help it

If you want to have a taste of the real life of the old Wild West, go to a rodeo. These shows have grown out of the day-to-day working skills a good cattleman must learn. Now, many of the competing cowboys are professionals who travel from one rodeo to another, but there is still a place for amateurs to have a go, and all the unexpectedness and excitement of the various sports still exists.

There are five main sports in the world of rodeo: cutting, calf roping, bronc riding, steer wrestling or bulldogging, and chuck wagon racing. There are other events, too, such as bull riding, wild cow milking and the wild horse race. They each need a different skill; they all demand courage, timing, strength.

Really top-class cutting horses are very valuable. In a cutting competition, one animal must be separated from the herd and kept apart from it by the horse. It is rather like the task of a sheepdog in isolating one of the flock. The rider selects a steer and manoeuvres it away from the herd, but after that he must drop the reins–the rest is up to the horse. Quarter Horses, renowned for their intelligence and agility, make the best cutting horses. The horse has to out-think the steer, anticipating what it will do and out-manoeuvring it by a mixture of instinctive 'steer-sense' and nimble movements. Though the rider is not allowed to help, he has to be a skilled horseman in order to keep perfectly in balance with his horse all the time.

Like cutting work, calf roping has always been an important skill. How else, for example, can you catch your calf in order to brand it with the ranch brand mark? Good roping horses are also highly prized, and there aren't very many of them. The calf comes into the arena, trips over an automatic timing wire and rushes on. The cowboy, whirling his lariat in true dramatic style–but for a purpose, too!–pursues the calf and eventually lassoos it, which is a very tricky thing to do. As soon as the noose is over the calf's head the horse begins to take the strain, coming to a rapid halt and pulling backwards to keep the rope taut. At the same time, the rider leaps off and runs to the calf, tying three of its legs together with a 'pigging string'. If the calf remains tied up for six seconds, the competitor has succeeded, and the rest depends on how his time taken compares with the others.

Bronc riding is exhilarating to watch and can be hazardous to experience. Timing is again what matters: can you sit a violently leaping, twisting, bucking horse whose one idea is to dislodge you? Ten seconds–or eight seconds for some events–can seem a very long time when you are trying to sit it out. There are two kinds of bronc riding: bareback, when the horse wears nothing but a surcingle with a handle attached, and the buckstrap; and saddle bronc riding, when the horse has saddle and stirrups, and a stout halter with rope attached. In either case, only one hand is allowed to hold on with, staying put is rarely possible, and if you do manage to last long enough, you then have the problem of how to get off!

If you find bronc riding a bit tame–and few do–then you could try bull riding, which can be positively dangerous. Again one-handed, the rider clings to a rope tied round the bull's belly. Once he hits the ground–on purpose or by mistake–he must leap to his feet and run for the barrier, for there is a good chance that the bull will turn on him. In bronc riding, there will be mounted pickup men in the arena to lend a helping hand; in bull riding, there is also a clown, a brave and highly skilled man whose baggy-panted, funny appearance is secondary to his ability to distract the bull without getting hurt himself.

First-rate co-ordination between horse and rider is important not only in cutting and calf roping competitions but also for steer wrestling. Here, galloping alongside a steer, the rider leans right out of the saddle, grabs the steer's horns and hurls himself out of the saddle on to the steer, which he must try to bring to the ground. If the horse falters or swerves, he will just land on the ground with a humiliating bump.

Chuck wagon races began as a hell-for-leather ride back to town by the round-up wagons at the end of a round-up. Now, the wagons are stripped down so they are as light as possible, and are drawn by a team of four Thoroughbreds, racing fit. Each wagon is accompanied by four outriders, who load up the wagon with a tent, poles and a cooking stove before leaping onto their own horses and following the wagon in hot pursuit, flanking it in the mad gallop round the racetrack.

Rodeos are familiar and frequent entertainments in America and Canada, and with the increasing popularity of Quarter Horses, are now becoming popular in Australia, too. Each event is a real test of strength and skill, and a great source of pride to the men who succeed.

An Alphabetical Quiz

A	Some of these are natural, others artificial	**N**	It shouldn't be necessary to use one of these if your pony's saddle fits properly
B	You could ride without one, but might find it difficult to stop	**O**	Too many will probably make your pony hot up
C	A small jump used in training	**P**	A kind of bit
D	A useful brush, but not one for tender or ticklish places	**Q**	An American breed named after a special kind of race
E	This British breed is named after the area the wild herds live in	**R**	If your pony bucks, you may feel you are taking part in one of these
F	Part of a pony's foot—and it doesn't croak!	**S**	You put your feet in them, but they are not shoes
G	It is fun to compete at these	**T**	You can tell your pony s age by looking at them, if you know how
H	An English type of horse with very high-stepping action	**U**	Head and toes should both be—
I	The Connemara pony's home	**V**	A doctor for animals
J	They ride racehorses	**W**	Made with hay, and good for massaging ponies' muscles
K	It's like a wet, rather sticky jelly, and very good for keeping leather soft	**X**	He was born in 430 BC, and wrote the first book on riding that we know about
L	A disease ponies get when they are allowed to eat too much rich grass	**Y**	It's a poisonous plant and could make your pony very ill
M	One of these made with bran makes a super treat for your pony	**Z**	It's rather like a horse, but has a stripey coat

Debbie Johnsey's Page

My Most Awful Moment

It was my first season, and just one month before Wembley. I was jumping on Mystery at the Romsey Show in the qualifying rounds for the Leading Junior Show Jumper of the year. Everything was going fine and we were jumping clear, when all of a sudden Mystery carried right on into the next fence and went straight through it instead of over! I landed up with one of the poles under my leg, a pole and Mystery on top and the most dreadful pain in my knee, rather like the kind of pain you get when you hit your funnybone hard, but hundreds of times worse. All I could think was, 'Oh! I shan't be able to ride at Wembley!' When they got me and the fence and Mystery all untangled I had to have my breeches cut off and they discovered I had a fractured knee. I was put to bed for a week, swathed in the most enormous bandages, but after another week I was hopping about on crutches, and two weeks later still I was allowed to ride again – very much strapped up, but very happy, too.

My Happiest Moment

No doubt about what that was! It was that year in the Junior European Open Championships at the moment when I realised that I had actually won! I think it was the only time that I have ever felt like crying because I was so happy.

The First Race I Ever Won

It was a sack race! I was riding my super little pony, Silver, who knew exactly what to do. She streaked off like the wind and stopped in just the right place for me to slip off her back right into the sack.

That pony was terrible when I first had her. For some reason she wouldn't go more than about 50 yards in the field – there was a peg that she just wouldn't go past. Eventually by sheer willpower, plus a bit of kicking, I managed to get her to do what I wanted and after that we had no trouble.

The first jumping that I won was on Stephen in some hunter trials. In fact it was the first time I had ever entered for any jumping and I was joint First in the pairs and Third in the big class.

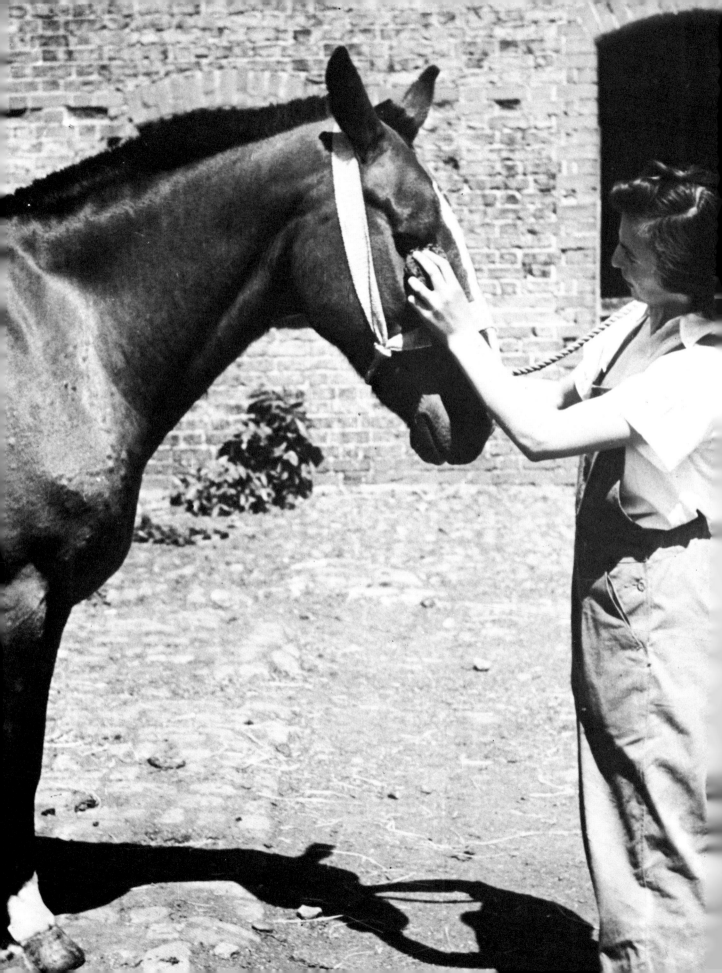

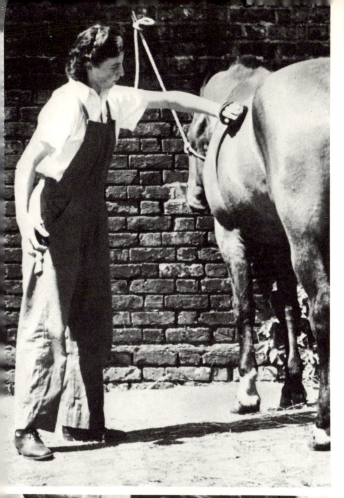

Looking after Your Pony

by Candida Geddes

Most ponies are quite happy on a diet of grass and not much else. But this does not mean that you can put a pony in a handkerchief-sized field and forget about it. A pony out at grass needs three acres to himself, and if you plan to keep more than one pony, a bigger area will obviously be needed. The grass must be kept in good condition, which involves resting part of the field part of the time, giving the grass a good rake and a roll every now and again, fertilising it with chemical fertilisers, and making sure it is adequately drained. Before you put your pony in a new field, inspect the field carefully to make sure there are no poisonous plants or shrubs in it, that the fencing is secure and safe—safe so that the pony can't damage himself on it, not only that he can't get out. A fence made up of a rusty bedstead and some rope is *not* a fence!

The pony must have a constant supply of fresh water. A bucket is too easily knocked over, so make sure there is a trough (with no sharp and damaging edges) either with piped water supplied to it, or one that can be filled from a garden hose. Keep the water clean, as ponies are fussy about water and will often go thirsty rather than drink water which is stale and dirty.

The amount of grass and the goodness it contains obviously varies depending on the time of year. In winter, from September onwards, the pony will need to have hay, even if it is not in work. If you are working your pony you will need to supplement his diet with concentrated feeds. Oats tend to make ponies too excitable. The best kind of food is pony nuts, about 3 lb a day, and 1 lb of bran as well. Always damp bran with a little water before giving it to the pony. At any time, your pony will probably enjoy being given a change of diet; beware, though, of feeding him large quantities of unsuitable titbits. If you want to give him a reward, give him an apple (not a whole one, cut it up into pieces or he may choke) or pieces of carrot. Do not feed him household scraps, lots of bread and sugar lumps. They are not good for him.

Grooming: left, *gently sponging the eyes;* top right, *how to use the body brush;* lower right, *the best way of brushing out the tail, a few hairs at a time*

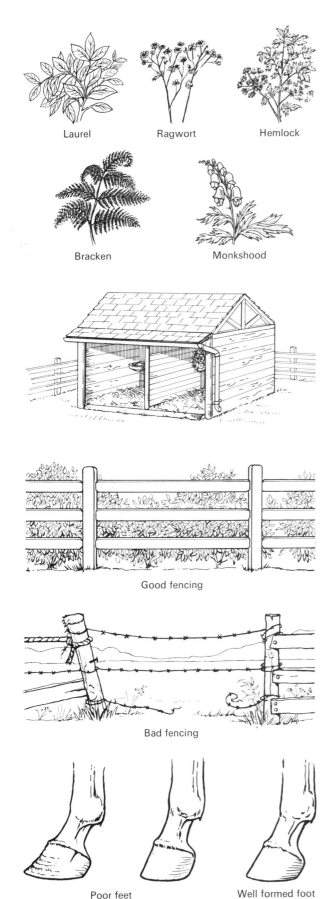

Laurel

Ragwort

Hemlock

Bracken

Monkshood

Good fencing

Bad fencing

Poor feet

Well formed foot

In the summer there is a danger of the pony scoffing so much of the good, rich grass that he becomes rotund. An unfit, puffing pony is not much fun to ride, and the strain of a rider on his back when he is himself overweight and with slack muscles can do quite a lot of damage. If your pony is fat and unfit, ride him gently and cut down on his consumption of food until he becomes slimmer, fitter and more energetic. There is a very painful disease called laminitis which overweight ponies are prone to. If you think your pony is getting too fat, you must either bring him into a stable and not let him eat anything for part of the day, or fence off a corner of the field and put him in this enclosed area for a while. Always make sure that there is some shelter from sun and flies and that water is available to him.

Even if you are not riding your pony every day, you should make sure he is visited by somebody to make sure that he is all right. Ponies that are ignored for long periods on end can also forget what good behaviour towards humans is like, and will become less friendly and co-operative.

The amount of work you give your pony will depend not only on how much free time you have, but also on what you want the pony to be able to do. It is no good leaving a pony in a field and then suddenly expecting him to be ready to carry you for a day out hunting, or compete in a gymkhana. So ride him as regularly as you can for hacking and picnics and other outings, and also give him schooling sessions. Keep schooling sessions short; about half an hour a day will be enough if you both concentrate and work hard. When you are out riding you can put into practice the schooling lessons you are working on. Some people think that one sort of riding belongs in the school, and once away from the school you can ride all anyhow and it doesn't matter. That is nonsense. A well-balanced, handy, obedient pony who responds promptly to his rider's aids will be more *fun* to ride as well as being a 'better' pony.

You will want to take pride in your pony's appearance and make sure he looks clean and smart when you take him out for a ride. Remember one thing, though. In winter, the pony's coat will have quite a lot of grease in it which acts as extra protection against the weather. Too much grooming will remove the grease. So, in winter you should just

Your pony's field: watch out for poisonous plants like those shown here; a dry, solidly-built shelter will protect your pony from flies, wind and rain; make sure the fencing is not only secure but safe for the pony, too

48

give the pony a going over with the dandy brush to remove mud from his coat, brush out his mane and tail with the body brush and pick out his feet. That is enough. If you are going to a gymkhana in summer – in fact at any time during the summer, when the coat is not needed for protection – then you can give your pony the full treatment.

If you want your pony to be in full work during the winter, his long coat will be a nuisance, and it would be better to clip him and keep him stabled. A stabled pony, of course, needs a good deal more attention than a pony at grass. He must be thoroughly groomed and exercised every day, his stable must be cleaned out and cared for. An alternative is to trace clip the pony. A trace clip clips away the long hair under the pony's tummy to about halfway up his flanks and the underside of the neck. A trace clipped pony in a New Zealand rug, which is a specially lined, waterproof rug, can live happily outside, but he too will need proper daily attention.

Ponies are very seldom ill, but you should learn enough about first aid and about possible ailments and illnesses to know when the vet should be called. Scratches should be washed clean and possibly covered with antiseptic ointment. If your pony goes completely off his food, something is wrong and it is probably wisest to call the vet. If he goes lame, check his feet to make sure no stone has got lodged in, and that his shoes are comfortable and not worn out. A word about shoeing: unless you are only going to ride on very soft ground, it is best to have your pony shod. He will need to have his shoes removed by the blacksmith and his feet trimmed once a month, and the shoes renewed at intervals. When you are cleaning out his feet, watch for raised 'clenches', as the nails are called, loose or worn shoes. You only have to think of the agony of wearing a pair of shoes that do not fit properly yourself, to appreciate the importance of taking good care of your pony's feet.

There is a lot of common sense in looking after ponies: don't spoil your pony, but look after him kindly and firmly. A pony is not a pet in the way a cat is. He needs firmness and someone he can respect, not somebody who lets him have his own way the whole time and then gets angry when he does something wrong. He will repay all your sensible, firm, kind care, though.

Stable management: learn how to tie up your pony with the quick-release knot shown on this page. A well-pulled mane and tail looks tidy, but get an expert to show you what to do. You will need all these in your grooming kit

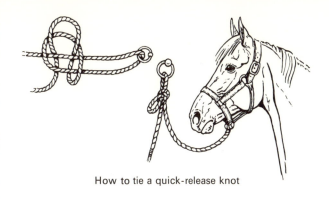

How to tie a quick-release knot

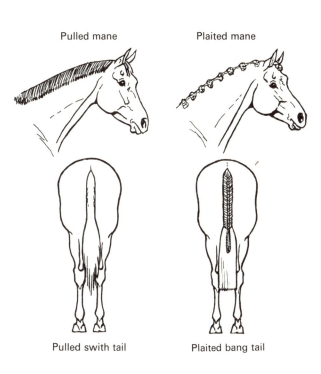

Pulled mane   Plaited mane

Pulled swith tail   Plaited bang tail

Dandy brush   Body brush   Water brush

Hoofpick

Rubber curry comb   Mane comb   Metal curry comb

Sweat scraper   Stable rubber   Sponge

SILVER'S FIRST RACE

a story from the book Silver Dollar
by Leslie W. Robinson

We moved up in a line, ready for the off. I managed to push Silver into a very favourable position, with only one horse between us and the rails, the rest of the field being bunched away on our right.

Just when I expected the tapes to go up, the horse on the left started to side into Silver in spite of his jockey's frantic efforts to keep out of our way, and when the animal's quarters smacked into the grey's ribs he didn't like it at all, immediately lashing out quite viciously with both hind legs at the intruder.

Then, just at this vital time, as I was wrestling with my horse, the tapes went up, and in that fraction of a second I was caught off balance, with the field having already sprung into action. I was left a good two lengths and so unable to get my usual flying start. Desperately I shouted at Silver:

"Get on there!"

This extract comes from a book that I think is really
exciting and enjoyable. The author, Mr Robinson,
sent me copy to read and I liked it so much that
I was determined to include a bit of it here.

I stuck my heels in him for all I was worth, and he was off like a streak of lightning, stretched out to catch up. We had lost valuable lengths, yet he flew over the ground at such a speed that just before the first hurdle was reached we were on the tail of a bunch of eight horses galloping almost abreast of each other. *Zip! Bang!* They were all up and over, followed closely by Silver, who, without slackening his speed for an instant, rose at the jump and, with a fantastic leap, landed safely, out-jumping by a good length two of the animals who had taken off beside him.

After this first burst I tried to slow him down, but in spite of my efforts he passed this rearguard of horses at a fast speed. Fortunately two of the horses ahead of us were away out in front of the others by a good ten lengths' lead, streaking round the bottom bend as if they were jet-propelled. I thought what silly things they must be; in a long-distance hurdle race they would never last out the finish at the speed they were going.

We swept round the bend into the eastern stretch, Silver tracking on the rails. He cleared the next two hurdles superbly and I was pleased to feel that he was not 'jumping big' or leaving too much daylight. As we passed the stands three other jockeys were racing almost level with us on our right. Out of the corner of my eye I saw that the nearest was Crystal Spring. This was the one I had to watch!

The whole field was going at a stiff racing gallop when we entered the western straight, with the two leaders away out in front and setting up a terrific pace. I felt Silver's long racing stride beginning to take him past the horses on our right. He had obviously spotted the leaders, for he pulled at me like a runaway, straining to increase his speed and go after them. With my left hand I gripped the leather strap around his neck that was attached to the checking nose-band and, without jerking, smoothly but firmly exerted a gradual pressure, so that the straps running above his nostrils were pulled down. Silver took exception to this attempt to put a brake on his mad gallop, and without slackening his stride he defiantly jerked up his head, giving my left arm a tremendous wrench. But whether he liked it or not I persisted in this treatment until it had the desired effect and we continued to race side by side with the field, sweeping round the bottom bend into the eastern straight, taking the two hurdles, and coming into the top bend practically neck to neck. I was still racing tight on the rails with my riding boot almost touching. "If Silver swerves by so much as an inch," I thought, "I've had it." But Fate was kind. We got safely round, all bunched up one on top of the other.

Then the next hurdle loomed up. We rose to it and again every horse was over. Silver put in such a leap that it gained for him a good advantage over the rest of the field, and I was perturbed to find that we were now leading the whole cavalcade with the exception of the two front tear-aways. I gave Silver another firm pull on the strap. My left arm was aching terribly and was beginning to go numb, but I dared not relax my grip.

Hard at it we thundered at breakneck speed down the long straight and met the next hurdle racing out on our own from the main bunch. With a clear view Silver made no bones about this jump, which he took like a stag, not losing an inch. I kept my position, straining and sweating, my knees tightly gripping the forward flaps of the saddle.

On we went at a cracking gallop until the bottom bend came in view. By this time the two front jockeys were beginning to reap the fruits of their tear-away tactics. Nevertheless they were already round the bend and plugging on gamely up the straight, though at a much reduced pace.

Silver swept round that last bend pulling like a ton of bricks. I was sitting quite happily, but, strange though it may seem, I could not help thinking even at this vital moment what huge eyes the grey had and how funny it was to see his breath shooting out from his nostrils. Quickly however my thoughts and energies were directed elsewhere, for at this stage we were approaching one of the last two hurdles, with a number of jockeys now banging up alongside the grey, their whips and arms flaying, all urging their mounts on to greater efforts. But I had not made my move yet, still sitting there with my feet well forward, holding Silver in with all my strength; the time had not come for me to make my challenge. Moreover, the two favourites had not shown themselves on the scene. But, I was not left long in the dark on this point. Glancing to my right I now saw Crystal Spring right up alongside me and going extremely well. About a length behind was Maharajah Slipper, the second favourite. They rose to the hurdle with the grey right on their tails, and the three of us were safely over.

The two pace-makers had now painfully spent their force, and we three passed them as if they were standing still. Crystal Spring was now leading Maharajah Slipper by a good length and striding out, looking all over the winner; but Silver was still there, hanging on grimly to their tails, and although I knew that the crucial moment of the race was at hand, I was still not perturbed, as I could feel that my horse would only need the urging to go up to them and make his challenge. This time had not quite come, so I sat there right behind them with Silver pulling double.

The last hurdle. Crystal Spring rose to it, jumping splendidly, and was over, with Maharajah Slipper just a fraction behind. Then Silver rose to it and was over too. By this time we could hear the shouting and roaring of the crowds in the stands. Crystal Spring was still in the lead, with Maharajah Slipper gallantly holding on for a close second with Silver sweating it out, still two lengths behind. The winning post was in sight, with two hundred yards to go.

This was the moment I had waited for. You can't come without the horse, but this was Silver Dollar's day.

"Come on, Silver!" I shouted. "Let her go!"

With arms and legs pushing him on I set him alight. He needed no urging; back went his ears and, stretching out with his great stride, he was instantly up with and past Maharajah Slipper, leaving only Crystal Spring to head and pass. His rider, on seeing the grey coming up to pass him with the race almost won, put in every ounce of strength and expert riding ability to keep Silver at bay, but without effect. Silver's strength of finish immediately brought him up level and, still hugging the rails, raced past, inch by inch with just twenty-five yards to go.

"Keep going, my beauty!" I shouted.

And we swept on to victory, a length in front of a gallant Crystal Spring.

Horses of America

The Appaloosa, originally ridden and bred by the Nez Percé Indians

In North America vast herds of horses established themselves as a result of the invasion of the continent in the sixteenth century by the Conquistadores of Spain. Later importation of bloodstock from the East, Europe and Great Britain helped the development of the various breeds, now famous in their turn in many other parts of the world.

One of the most useful of the American breeds is the Quarter Horse. It got its name from the races held at the end of the day's work by the stockmen, who rode at top speed down the quarter-mile-long main street of their local town. Selective breeding has made sure that the Quarter Horse is still the world's fastest over this distance.

The Quarter Horse is an immensely powerful and yet agile horse. The breed is still considered to be the best for working with cattle, as their intelligence and strength enable them to deal with them – twisting, turning, leaping into a gallop from a standstill – with great efficiency.

Quarter Horses are not very big – they average between 14.3 and 15.1 hands, though occasionally they go as large as 16 hands or even more. A good horse will have a short head, well developed jaw, muscled neck, a wide, deep chest giving plenty of room for heart and lungs. The legs are muscled but not at all coarse, and the hindquarters particularly powerful. It is important for the Quarter Horse to have well formed hocks, strong pasterns and good feet, for the work these horses do asks a lot of their legs, which must not strain easily.

It is the strength in the quarters and hind legs which help to make the Quarter Horse so valuable as a jumper, especially when it is crossed with, say, Thoroughbred blood. Quarter Horses are much the

most popular breed in the United States for all sorts of competitions, from polo to cowhorse classes, and they are also exported to many parts of the world.

The American Paint Horse, not to be confused with the Pinto (which just means a coloured horse, rather than being a proper breed) is a cousin of the

This horse's tack, and the way it is being ridden, are both in true Western style

Quarter Horse. Careful breeding control has eliminated the rather weedy horses that were sometimes found, and now a good Paint Horse looks rather like the Quarter Horse, apart from its colouring, of course.

There are two main types of colouring for the Paint: the Tobiano, which is predominantly white with large patches of colour on chest, head and flanks while the back is probably all-over white without markings; and the Overo, which is the opposite – a mainly solid coloured horse with splashes of white, mostly on the mid-section of its body, but seldom across the back. Paints can also be black, bay, sorrel, dun, palomino and roan in colour.

The Paint is also a very versatile horse, which is one reason why it is so popular. It can compete with the Quarter Horse in competitions such as roping, cutting, speed events, etc., and is also successful in the rodeo arena, where its skill and speed in calf-roping and bulldogging will always win admiration from the crowd.

The Standardbred was founded as a breed by a Thoroughbred stallion imported from England in the eighteenth century. Harness racing was popular in those days, and races at country fairs would always be held for those with fast horses. The winners were those whose horses came first in the most heats, and only these successful ones were considered good enough to be used as breeding stock. The English Thoroughbred, Messenger, was used for breeding Thoroughbreds, too, but it was the result of crossing his blood with that of the harness horses that really fast trotters began to compete. And from this modest beginning, the Standardbred breed was established.

A fine example of a Quarter Horse. This one was bred in Australia from an American sire

The Standardbred's appearance is similar to that of the Thoroughbred, but it has rather heavier bones and is somewhat less refined. Although they were first bred as harness horses, the Standardbreds also make good horses for riding and are excellent for endurance riding, where their determination and toughness are a great advantage.

Standardbreds are popular as pacers (horses whose legs move in lateral rather than diagonal pairs) as well as trotters, and are exported to all the countries where harness racing is popular, for at this sport they are hard to beat.

The Walking Horse earned its name from the unique smoothness of its two walking gaits – the flatfoot walk and the running walk. The breed grew from the blood of Standardbred, Thoroughbred, Morgan and Saddlebred horses, each of which gave the Walker its own best quality. The Walking Horses used to be most in demand on the huge cotton and tobacco plantations of the southern states, for the exceptionally comfortable ride they give enabled the owners of these vast plantations to ride their land all day.

Perhaps the strangest thing about the Morgan is that just one man, Justin Morgan, was responsible for the existence of the breed. Mr Morgan accepted

a horse named Figure as payment for a debt. Figure was remarkable; he would not only help in farmwork such as pulling heavy logs out from clearings but also won against all competition in match-racing, pulling and trotting contests. It was these successes that kept him in demand as a sire, and so special were his qualities that his offspring were almost all endowed with his versatility, strength and speed.

The Morgan has helped to shape the Standardbred, Saddlebred and Walking Horse breeds as well as being very popular in its own right. The Morgan is compact and muscular in appearance, though standing at only about 14 to 15 hands. It combines stamina and strength with gaiety and alertness.

The American Saddlebred is an elegant horse, the result of breeding from the best of Thoroughbred, Morgan, Standardbred and Naragansett Pacer blood. This breed has a high head and tail carriage, a refined and showy appearance, very smooth movements at all paces and great 'presence'. They were originally used as all-rounders for farm and saddle work, but have become very popular for the show ring and as parade horses as their appearance is so eye-catching.

Lastly, the Appaloosa, a horse of mixed origins, perhaps introduced into Spain in ancient times by the people of Asia. They reached America with Cortes and the Conquistadores, and found their way into the hands of the Nez Percé Indians, who lived in an area round the river Palouse, where the Appaloosa's name comes from. The Indians evidently knew about good breeding methods, for they sold off the poorer horses and only kept the best ones for themselves and as breeding stock. The Nez Percé needed horses with stamina and speed for hunting and for their wars with other tribes, horses that were sure-footed, calm enough to face elk and buffalo, docile enough to come to their masters even though they roamed free in that unfenced land.

Though the Nez Percé were defeated by the United States Army (cowboys and Indians, or at any rate, soldiers against Indians, are not just good story-lines for Westerns!) there was a revival of interest in the Appaloosa breed in the 1930s. Now, in common with the other American breeds, the Appaloosa has an Association to guard its interests and to maintain the quality of the breed.

Opposite is a Tennessee Walking Horse. The picture shows the unusual carriage of the tail

The Spanish Riding School in Vienna

Why a *Spanish* riding school in Austria's capital city? In the fifteenth and sixteenth centuries a breed of horses from Spain, the Andalusian, was very popular in other royal courts in Europe–among them the Viennese. The Lippizaner breed comes from these Andalusians, and only the best white Lippizaner stallions are trained at the Spanish Riding School.

The School itself is a splendid building which has been used since 1735, in the reign of the Emperor Charles VI. There's a portrait of him hanging in the hall, and every morning the riders raise their hats to him before beginning work.

Many of the movements practised by the School were first used at war. Imagine being a foot-soldier and finding a big, strong horse approaching you on its hind legs, as in the Capriole, or leaping into the air and kicking out with its hind legs before landing! These are just two of the 'airs above the ground', classical dressage movements taught only to the very best stallions at the School.

Lippizaners are the only horses trained at the School. They are specially bred at the Piber stud in Austria, and only the grey stallions are used. The foals' coats can be almost any colour, and they only turn the almost-white grey colour when they are about seven years old. It takes four or five years to train the Lippizaners, for their training must be done especially gradually. The actual training period is only 45 minutes a day.

Some of the movements are performed individually, both with a rider and also by the horse between pillars with his trainer on the ground. There is also a beautiful display by a dozen horses and riders of the School.

The Spanish Riding School is famous all over the world for the high standards it maintains in the oldest form of proper horsemanship.

These horses are wonderful. I went to see them when I was at the Vienna Show. Top left, the pas de deux; *right, the quadrille; lower left, a magnificent* capriole *and, right, the impressive strength shown in the* levade

Ponies of Britain

Ponies have been living in Britain for many hundreds of years. Until quite recently they have bred by themselves; in other words, men did not interfere by trying (sometimes, of course, succeeding) to improve the breed. Ponies lived in the wild, and the best ones were those which lived healthily and went on to breed more ponies. This is called 'natural selection', and means that in time the standard of the whole breed is very high. Herds in the different areas of Britain have not mingled with each other, but even so there are some characteristics which belong to all of them, and indeed to all ponies in other parts of the world too. Ponies are often more intelligent than horses, perhaps because they have had to cope without any help; they are usually very healthy and hardy, with fairly thick winter coats to help them get through snowy and icy winters without being too miserable or catching cold; they are sure-footed and capable of looking after themselves. In fact, the typical characteristics of ponies have proved so valuable that they are now often used in the breeding of horses. A mixture of pony toughness and good sense and the speed and conformation of, for example, a Thoroughbred, can produce some of the best ponies – or horses – of all.

This colour photograph of the herd of Welsh ponies was taken in Wales; there are four Welsh breeds. In black and white, from the top, is a Highland pony, an all-rounder from Scotland; the Dales, who comes from the Pennines and is used for driving and riding; the small, hardy Exmoor with his mealy muzzle and a lovely Connemara from Ireland. Turn the page and you will find, left, *Dartmoors, intelligent, handsome and ideal for children;* right, *Welsh Mountains, smallest and most beautiful of the Welsh breeds; and,* below, *the smallest of all British ponies, the lovable Shetlands*

Pony Quiz

Britain's native ponies are the most famous in the world, and are now exported to many other countries and are being bred there too. Do you know whereabouts in Britain each breed comes from? Put a number beside each of the names listed here, to correspond with the numbers shown on the map. You'll find out whether you're right by looking up the answers on page 77.

Fell
Connemara
New Forest
Shetland
Welsh
Dartmoor
Highland
Exmoor
Dales

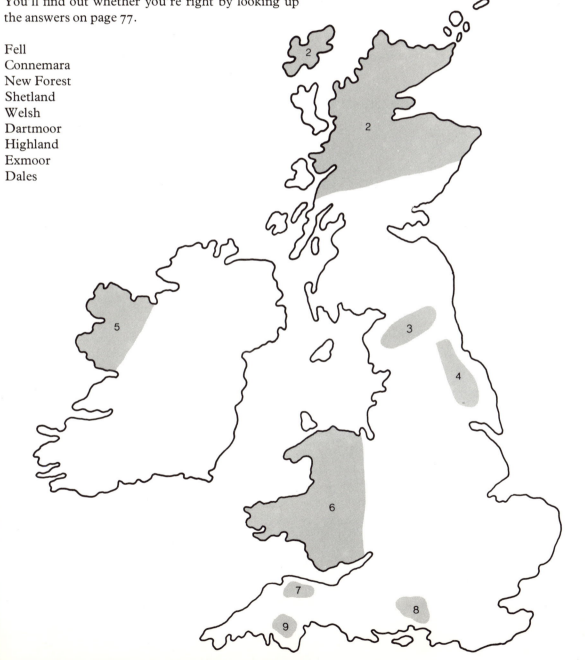

BRONCO

a story by Carol Vaughan

Here's the other Western I told you about—it is a super story

"They can't have him! They just can't!" shouted Jeff Lyons, trying to climb into the corral as the sorrel stallion circled nervously, watching the man with the lariat with wild eyes.

"We must have some cash," said Nora Lyons, trying again to make Jeff understand. "Pa may not be back for a month from his business trip and I can't sell any of the other stock. He always said the sorrel would only be any use for a rodeo; no one can ride him."

"But I have," cried Jeff. "I've been working on him ever since Pa left. He'll come to me now. I've ridden him in the corral with just a halter. Let me go! They can't have him!"

But it was too late. The lariat snaked out round the neck of the fighting sorrel stallion and Ed Green, the horse-dealer who specialised in buying bucking horses for the rodeos, was dragging his new purchase away.

Jeff woke up, his desperate cry still ringing in his ears, and sat up dazedly. It was a year now since the sorrel had gone, but he still dreamed often of that last day. And if they could have held out for another two weeks they could have kept the stallion; Rod Lyons had returned at last with his money belt sagging, news of money in the bank and a bright new life for them all on the big ranch they were going to buy farther west. Jeff had the choice of fifty horses now; he could ride anything on the ranch, but none of them could match the sorrel stallion. That last morning the horse had greeted him with a whinny when he ran down to the corral, had come up freely and dropped his nose into the boy's familiar, welcoming hands. Haltering him, Jeff had mounted and ridden round the corral with nothing more than a rebellious snort from the proud, wild horse.

"We're going into town today," said Rod Lyons at breakfast, with a secret grin at his wife. Jeff saw the grin but he did not guess what it meant until they reached the town and saw the crowds, the flags in the streets and the big banner stretched across the main street, RODEO TODAY.

"A rodeo!" exclaimed Jeff, his heart leaping with sudden hope.

"We reckoned you'd like that," said Rod Lyons, grinning broadly. "Haven't been to one for quite a while myself."

"Do you think..." began Jeff, but he couldn't finish. His father was not listening, leaning out to talk to a passing friend, but his mother sighed. She knew that Jeff had never forgotten the sorrel stallion.

64

The seats around the arena were half filled already with a shouting, laughing crowd, but the animals in the corrals looked half asleep. Jeff searched through the herd of bucking horses, but he could not see one which could be the sorrel horse. The seats were filling up fast as people crowded in, trying to find their friends, clumping on the wooden boards of the stands until they swayed so dangerously that Jeff's mother wondered if they were safe—but they had been lucky, their seats were fairly close and on a gangway, so they could get out easily.

The announcer came out and the noise in the stands died to a murmur as he announced the first event. Jeff could hardly wait for the Bronco Riding Contest, hoping against hope that he might have missed the sorrel stallion. He watched horse after horse burst out of the chutes, screwing itself up into an incredible tangle of arching back and flailing legs, but they were all strangers to him. As the winner, a cowboy who looked permanently bent from bronco-riding, stepped down with his prize, the announcer called for silence with a lifted hand.

"Now, folks, you'll be glad to hear that there's a Surprise Event this afternoon, not on your programme. It's not often we have an offer like this, but we have here this afternoon the famous bucking horse, Red Riot. You'll all have heard of this horse, I guess. Now, anyone who wants to volunteer to ride this horse for 10 seconds—only 10 seconds, folks," he added, waiting for the burst of laughter from the crowd which knew the hazards of trying to stay aboard for eight seconds—"has the chance to win $5,000 cash—or can have the horse as a gift," he added, waiting again for the crowd's roar of laughter. Who'd want an outlaw bronco? "Now, I don't want to rush you. We'll be open to offers right through the afternoon. Just step along to the corral and we'll fix you up. Roll up, boys, no hanging back there." Again the crowd laughed, but there was no mad rush to ride Red Riot. They were mostly local cowboys competing and it would take a professional bronco rider to tackle a horse like that.

"There's Chet Preston going over," said Rod Lyons. "He always was crazy."

Beaming, the announcer, one hand on Chet Preston's shoulder, urged him forward for everyone to see. "Now, here's one guy's got the guts," he cried. "Well, folks, this is it. You are now going to see Chet Preston riding the West's most famous outlaw—Red Riot. Five thousand dollars or a horse of your own, what'll it be, Chet? He says he'll take the cash—if he can," roared the announcer jovially and the crowd rocked with laughter. "Now, this'll be a perfectly fair contest between man and horse. Red Riot will wear just a fine, strong halter, with a rope on it—guaranteed a good, tough rope, folks, no tricks to that. And you only have to stay on his back for ten seconds, Chet. That shouldn't worry a rider like you, should it?"

The cowboy grinned and walked off to the chute where the crowd could see the shape of a horse through the bars. They were not taking any chances with Red Riot; they had brought him in in a trailer and unloaded him directly into the chute. Lowering himself onto the gleaming, bare back, Chet grasped the rope firmly, but it didn't feel like much support for a battle with the bunching muscles beneath him. Everyone seemed to be holding their breath for a long, expectant moment and then the chute flew open and the horse exploded out into the arena, a whirling cloud of sorrel fury.

"It's him," shrieked Jeff. "It's the sorrel stallion." He was out of his seat and running down the steps before Chet Preston hit the ground—four seconds of that sort of bucking bronco had felt like a lifetime.

"Jeff!" shouted his mother, jumping to her feet, but she was too late. Jeff was already climbing the high fence and running towards the stallion as Chet Preston picked himself up, grinning ruefully, the crowd groaning with exaggerated sympathy.

"Easy there, fella," said Jeff, slowing to a walk and stopping a few feet from the stallion, who was eyeing him curiously, half turned away and ready to bolt. "Now, don't go tearing off again. This is your only chance. Easy, now." His hand reached out for the dangling halter rope and the horse snorted. Carefully Jeff moved closer, unaware that the crowd was watching him in dead silence.

The sorrel stallion's nostrils flared, his eyes watching the boy suspiciously, ready to explode backwards. But this one was different. That voice. That hand. It stirred his memory. Lowering his nose he just touched the outstretched hand with stiff whiskers before jerking back again, but the hand had not moved and he sniffed it again, curiously, Jeff willing him to remember. The horse *had* to remember. If he'd forgotten...

"Come on," said Jeff, turning away almost carelessly, hiding his fear that the rope would be snatched out of his hand. "Come on over here. I've got to ride you if you want to come home." He dared not vault onto the horse's back; the sudden movement would be fatal. Leading him to the arena fence, one hand on the satin-smooth, hard-muscled neck, talking all the time in the voice the stallion might remember, Jeff climbed up two rungs. Holding his breath, he slid onto the powerful back and sat, stroking the horse's neck for nearly a minute—far longer than the time demanded by the announcer—before he touched the horse with his heels and pressed the rope against his neck, urging him away from the fence. Sitting on him might not be enough. He had to ride him to prove his right to the horse—for five thousand dollars, but that never crossed his mind.

The sorrel stallion, eyes rolling uneasily, ears stiffly suspicious, almost as unbelieving as the watching crowd, walked slowly round the arena, the boy absolutely still on his back, broke into a trot and crossed the arena at a canter, stopping in a few short strides at the fence. Jeff slipped to the ground and stood stroking the horse's neck, talking to him, as the announcer came hurrying across the arena, Red Riot's startled owner and Jeff's parents at his heels.

Jeff never remembered much about that scene. The stallion wouldn't stand so many people that close and he led him away as the owner shook Rod Lyons' hand, congratulating him, with a look of dazed astonishment on his son's skill with horses, and offering him a thick wad of notes—five thousand dollars.

But Rod Lyons shook his head, looking pretty dazed himself. "I guess Jeff doesn't want that," he said. "You want the stallion, don't you, son?"

Jeff nodded and grinned, slipping his hand up over the horse's wary, snorting nostrils. His horse.

Train Your Pony for Jumping

by Candida Geddes

Perhaps the most important thing of all to remember is that if your pony can be taught to *enjoy* jumping, he will probably jump well. If he doesn't like it, you will both get cross and impatient. Teach him slowly, and be firm but kind.

The best way to start is by walking him over poles on the ground on a loose rein. then you can raise the poles a few inches from the ground, and walk and trot over these. It is important that the poles are the right distance apart for your pony's stride, and you may need some help with adjusting them. If your pony gets over-excited and tries to rush at the line of cavalletti (as these training poles are called), bring him back to a calm walk before you try again.

It can be a good idea to train your pony when there aren't any other ponies around to distract him, but in some ways it is more fun if you can school him with friends. If you are with other ponies, make sure that yours will jump when he is going away from the others, not just when he is facing them.

Once your pony has begun to understand what you want him to do, look out for small things to jump when you are out on a ride. How about a fallen log, or a pig trough, sheep rack, or even the draining ditches on the verge of the road? Your pony can easily jump fences as low as this almost from a standstill, so you don't need to give him a long approach to the fence. If he is feeling unco-operative, he will probably run out. So bring him round to the fence quite close to it, and make sure you approach it straight, not at an angle. If he stops, turn him round, take him back only a few strides and try again.

If your pony is to enjoy jumping, you must make sure that you are helping him rather than making his job more difficult. Lean slightly forward as you come up to the fence, and give a little with your hands on take-off. Whatever happens, make sure that you do not jab him in the mouth on landing, and try to land back in the saddle gently.

Constructing fences at home can be fun. Try to make the fences look solid rather than flimsy. A pony soon learns when it is easier to go through rather than over! Only jump for about half an hour at a time, even if you feel like jumping all day.

When your pony will trot freely over cavalletti, it is good for both of you to practise exercises for suppleness and balance, as in the two top photographs on this page. Giving a pony jumping lessons on the lunge teaches him to jump freely before having to cope with the rider's weight. The pictures on the right show (below) a nice ordinary pony and rider schooling on a circle, and (above) a happy combination jumping well and confidently in the ring

Trekking and Endurance Riding

One of the best ways for an inexperienced rider to enjoy a relaxing ride in beautiful countryside is to go pony trekking; one of the most rewarding ways for an experienced rider to prove the fitness of himself and his horse and also to ride through beautiful countryside, is to take part in an endurance ride. In other words, trekking and endurance riding are both similar and different.

It is a good idea for the would-be trekker to have a few lessons at a riding school before going trekking. But as most of the ride is at a walking pace, you need be no expert. The rides are planned to go through the nicest possible areas, so although you cannot go off and explore on your own, you can enjoy marvellous views, and get the feeling of freedom and exploration all the same. Trekking centres are almost always to be found in parts of the country recognised as specially worth seeing.

Endurance riding is a particularly popular sport in the United States, where there are a number of hundred-mile rides lasting three days, and the most famous ride, the Tevis Cup, where you have to cover 100 miles in just one day. One of the good things about endurance riding is that you do not need to have an expensive, highly trained horse in order to do well. What counts is the time and trouble put into the training of your horse—and yourself—

so that you are fit enough to be able to complete the ride without becoming completely exhausted. All endurance rides have veterinary checks before, during and after the ride to make sure each horse is still fit and well. The routes of the rides in the United States are chosen so that you ride through sand, over hills, rocky areas, every kind of country.

The most important ride in England, where endurance riding is now also becoming popular, is the Golden Horseshoe Ride, which is held over seventy-five miles. To enter, you have to qualify by completing one of the shorter rides held in various parts of the country earlier in the year. Many people enter the qualifying rides for the fun of it without intending to go on to the Golden Horseshoe ride itself. In the Golden Horseshoe, competitors must ride fifty miles on the first day and twenty-five miles on the second. There are inspections by the vet for this ride, too, and he awards fitness points so the aim is not only to complete the ride, but to complete it with your horse in good condition at the end.

The Australian rides are also judged not only on the time taken to ride the course but also on the state of the horse when it reaches the finish. The sport has caught on very quickly in Australia, the most important ride being the Quilty Cup, a 100-mile ride held in the Blue Mountains, near Sydney.

Though you do not need to have a high-class horse to compete, it has been found that breeds known for their stamina do very well in these competitions. The Arab is most popular for endurance rides; in Australia, the Waler holds his own; in America the Quarter Horse and the Appaloosa often win awards, and in Britain Thoroughbreds, native pony cross-bred animals, Welsh cobs have all had some success.

Working for a Living

You could say that a pony probably doesn't see the difference between one sort of work and another, and that being ridden or driven is all work, whether the humans involved are enjoying themselves or are working. Nevertheless, let's look at working ponies as though they could tell the difference, and see where they still help humans in their work.

Until not so long ago, ponies in many parts of the world were the only means of transport for thousands of farmers and peasant peoples, and for small

Cicero, the famous Guards' drum horse

traders in towns. Many tasks are now done by mechanical equipment, but there are still people who either can't afford the machines or who prefer to have ponies to help them. In many of the Mediterranean countries, ponies are still the maid of all work, and a very important member of the family. In countries like Canada, you will find them pulling sledges at a time of year when cars are likely just to get stuck in snowdrifts. In mountainous areas of the world, the nimble-footed, plodding, reliable pony can and will get to places no vehicle could reach. Ponies are still used by costermongers in London, and until quite recently were still helping with the milk round in towns–stopping of their own accord at each house while the milkman delivered the milk.

By some odd coincidence, riding for pleasure really became widespread only when ponies and

Beautiful shire horses in a ploughing match

horses were not strictly necessary any more. One result of this was the setting up of riding schools, where people who didn't have their own ponies could learn to ride and help to look after ponies. Now, thousands of ponies in Britain and in many other parts of the world too, work for their living in this new way.

Another new way in which ponies work is giving an enormous amount of fun to disabled children. Riding for the Disabled was started in Scandinavia some years ago, and now there are centres in places as far apart as New Zealand, Britain and the United States.

It seems that in some parts of the world machines will never replace the pony as a worker; and where they do, ponies become popular in other ways. So the ponies' future seems secure.

Police horses are trained to face anything

What the Judges Look For

by Candida Geddes

Taking your pony in to the show ring can provide a lot of fun, and give very useful experience in getting your pony to the peak of condition and learning how to make him look his best. Ponies specially bred for showing are now fantastically expensive, and will indeed be hard to beat, but do not be despondent if your pony doesn't look like any of the famous ones. A lot can be done at home

to improve your pony's appearance and a quite ordinary looking pony, well schooled and with the right rider, can go a long way.

Show pony classes are now usually very popular, and there are so many competitors in each class that it is very difficult for the judges to look at them all properly. If you want to do well, there are various points to remember which are likely to help you get the judge to notice you. Some of these—like making sure that your pony is obedient and doesn't get over-excited in company, that your tack is clean and in good condition, that your pony and yourself are beautifully groomed—need attention at home long before you get anywhere near the show ring. But there are also hints on how best to show your pony.

When you file in your turn from the collecting ring, make sure you leave a sensible distance between yourself and the pony in front of you. No judge can be expected to notice you if you are all bunched up together. At all stages, try to keep clear of other ponies.

Be alert. Watch the judge or, at the bigger shows, the stewards, for instructions to change pace. Don't anticipate their instructions, but if you are among the first to trot, say, you will notch up a good mark. If you are called in high enough up the line to be asked to give an individual show and to strip your pony for the judge's scrutiny, be ready to do as you are asked promptly.

We have mentioned obedience. Let's look into the judge's mind for a moment. What might he be thinking of as a class of ponies comes in to the ring? These are children's ponies, so they ought to be suitable for children to ride. A good judge will not give an award to a pony, however beautifully made, that bucks, rolls the whites of its eyes, tries to kick the other ponies, or otherwise misbehaves. There are very few ponies whose manners are always absolutely perfect—and in fact they would be pretty boring to ride—but your pony should be well schooled enough to know what discipline is, and to change pace and direction smoothly and without a fuss.

A judge is likely to notice for the wrong reasons a child who looks very insecure, a pony that is dirty and scruffy, and any other signs that enough trouble has not been taken to prepare the pony for the show.

When you are showing, or watching others do so, you may notice that the judge keeps the class trotting for quite a long time—much longer than he does for the walk or canter. This is because you can best tell how a pony moves at the trot. So, when you are schooling your pony, make sure that you give plenty of practice to the trot. It should be energetic, even, full of impulsion but well controlled. If your pony has any glaring faults of conformation, I fear that they will not escape the judge's eye at the trot, though you may be able to disguise them at a walk or canter.

What the judge is looking for depends to a certain extent on the kind of class you have entered. If he is looking at young children on leading reins, the judge will want to find reliability, calmness, a nice narrow conformation so the child does not look as though he is sitting on top of a barrel. A true show pony class will have more importance given to presentation, quality and strictly correct conformation, including the indefinable 'ponyness' which even Thoroughbred ponies should possess. In a working pony class, an ability to jump cleanly and well is also important. Working pony classes are in some ways the best to enter if your pony is a good all-rounder but perhaps not quite as beautifully made as the top-class show ponies need to be.

People who Help Me

by Debbie Johnsey

Father, Kevin, me, Clair and Lee.

Of course the person who helps me most of all is my father. For one thing, he knows all about horses and loves them as much as I do, so he can understand just how I feel. Then he watches me, not only at shows, but when I'm training and practising, and he can pick out faults in me or in the horse and help me to correct them right from the start. It's marvellous to know that he is always there for advice and help when I need it.

He helps me, too, with all the paper work, which sometimes seems to be almost endless, registering the ponies and horses, filling in entry forms, keeping records of injections, wormings and so on.

Somebody else who is very important is Frank Keirnan, who looks out for good young horses for me – these days one can only buy novices, and Frank has an absolutely marvellous eye for a potential winner. He found Assam for me and he found David Broome's Philco and lots of others.

I don't think most people realise quite how important the blacksmith is. Our blacksmith comes down once a month from Staffordshire and brings all his own equipment with him. Perhaps it sounds a bit odd that he comes all that way – although he does come to other stables near us – but the fact is that Speculator has funny feet! He sort of turns them over and walks on the outside edge of the hoof, so he has to wear specially built-up shoes –

rather like surgical shoes! – as otherwise he goes dreadfully stiff and can't jump properly. And this blacksmith is absolutely marvellous and shoes Speculator perfectly.

Then, of course, there is the groom, who looks after the horse like a nanny, sees it gets the right things to eat, keeps all the tack in perfect condition and sits up all night, if necessary, if the horse is ill.

And almost the most important person is the vet, of course, who comes at a moment's notice if there's a crisis.

One thing that makes me feel good is the thought that people are really interested and sympathetic and wish me luck. It is always a thrill to get a letter from some stranger sending good wishes or congratulating me on a success. Of course a lot of the letters I get are from children who have their own ponies and from others who are saving up to buy a pony for themselves, and they tell me all about their problems. One of the letters that pleased me most was from an old man of 80, who wrote a marvellous letter on the occasion that I came second to Ann Moore; and another came from a young soldier who was one of the arena party at the R.I.H.S. One policeman, who collects photographs of Welsh sportsmen wrote asking for my picture to put on his wall.

It's useful to have other people to clean the silver!

I do try to answer all the letters I get, though sometimes if one is just handed to me at a show or somewhere, it is apt to get mislaid and I really feel bad about not answering! So if you write to me and I don't answer please forgive me.

And now it's time to say Goodbye! I do hope you've enjoyed reading this book as much as I've enjoyed talking to you all.

This was taken when I was jumping at Hickstead in the Puissance jumping against Harvey Smith. I came second. The jumps finished at 6ft. 4in!

Answers to Quiz Questions

Saddles and Bits

1 Breaking bit with keys
2 Loose ring mullen mouth snaffle
3 Loose ring German mouth snaffle
4 Eggbutt snaffle
5 Fulmer cheek snaffle
6 Kimblewick
7 Mullen mouth Pelham
8 Dressage Weymouth bit and eggbutt bradoon
9 Loose cheek Weymouth bit and bradoon with double-link curb chain
10 All purpose saddle
11 Jumping saddle
12 Dressage saddle
13 Show saddle
14 Racing saddle
15 Military saddle

Alphabetical quiz

A Aids
B Bridle
C Cavalletti
D Dandy brush
E Exmoor
F Frog
G Gymkhanas
H Hackney
I Ireland
J Jockeys
K Kocholine
L Laminitis
M Mash
N Numnah
O Oats
P Pelham
Q Quarter Horse
R Rodeo
S Stirrups
T Teeth
U Up
V Veterinary surgeon ('vet')
W Wisp
X Xenophon (yes, it's a difficult one, but it wasn't easy thinking of *anything* horsy beginning with X!)
Y Yew
Z Zebra

The Native Ponies of Britain

3 Fell
5 Connemara
8 New Forest
1 Shetland
6 Welsh
9 Dartmoor
2 Highland
7 Exmoor
4 Dales

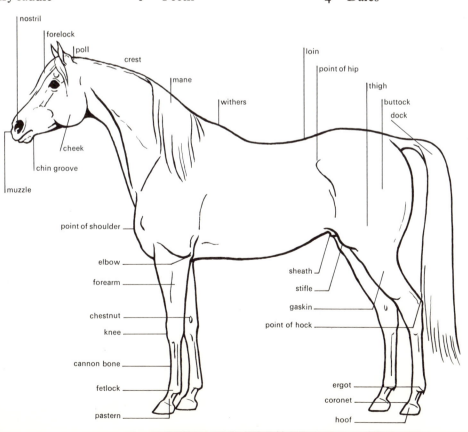

ISBN 0 7063 1663 0
First published in Great Britain 1975
by Ward Lock Limited, 116 Baker Street,
London, W1M 2BB

Designed by Brian Mayers Associates

Line Drawings by Christine Bousfield and
Joan Wankley

Text filmset in 10/12 pt Plantin
by London Filmsetters Limited

Made and Printed in Spain by
Heraclio Fournier S.A., Vitoria

The Publishers would like to thank the following
for permission to reproduce photographs and other
material in this book: Australian Information
Service; Australian News and Information Bureau;
Austrian National Tourist Office; K. Bright; Brunt:
The Commissioner of Metropolitan Police;
Clive Hiles; Keystone; E. D. Lacey; Leslie Lane;
Monty; Pictor; Pony and Light Horse; Pony
Magazine; Radio Times; Reuter; Mike Roberts;
Peter Roberts; South Wales Argus; Western
Americana.
The book, *Silver Dollar*, by Leslie W. Robinson,
is published by the Lady Gwendoline Publishing
Company, London.

In cases where it has been impossible to trace
the copyright holder, it is hoped that this
general acknowledgment will be acceptable.